RISE AND SHINE

FLORENCE YUWIMANA

authorHOUSE®

AuthorHouse™ UK
1663 Liberty Drive
Bloomington, IN 47403 USA
www.authorhouse.co.uk
Phone: UK TFN: 0800 0148641 (Toll Free inside the UK)
UK Local: (02) 0369 56322 (+44 20 3695 6322 from outside the UK)

© 2023 Florence Yuwimana. All rights reserved.

*No part of this book may be reproduced, stored in a retrieval system, or
transmitted by any means without the written permission of the author.*

Published by AuthorHouse 08/18/2023

ISBN: 979-8-8230-8385-0 (sc)
ISBN: 979-8-8230-8386-7 (hc)
ISBN: 979-8-8230-8387-4 (e)

Print information available on the last page.

*Any people depicted in stock imagery provided by Getty Images are models,
and such images are being used for illustrative purposes only.
Certain stock imagery © Getty Images.*

This book is printed on acid-free paper.

*Because of the dynamic nature of the Internet, any web addresses or links contained in
this book may have changed since publication and may no longer be valid. The views
expressed in this work are solely those of the author and do not necessarily reflect the
views of the publisher, and the publisher hereby disclaims any responsibility for them.*

CONTENTS

1 My Miracle Baby 1

2 Love Can Drive Out the Fear 11

3 Finding My Inner Strength 23

4 Happiness is not Based on What we Have 33

5 Facing a Mountain 43

6 Accepting the Love 53

7 Reaching Out 63

8 Learning to Smile Again 71

9 Rising from the Valley 79

10 Hope, the Mother of Success 87

1

MY MIRACLE BABY

The meaning of the name Florence is 'blossoming, flourishing and prosperous.' That is how I like to see my life now as a mother of three because my children bring me such joy. I was born on a different continent to where I now live, one of eight children, although sadly, one had passed away; now, I live across the world from my place of birth, where her daddy and I are raising our children.

Every new mother sees their baby as a miracle. My first baby brought that joy into our lives. I put my heart and soul into learning to become a mum, and I was so excited by the prospect of raising my beautiful daughter, looking forward

Florence Yuwimana

to all the mother/daughter chats we would share throughout the years.

Since discovering I was pregnant with our first child, my heart filled with true happiness. As the pregnancy progressed, my collection of nursery items grew. My heart's desire to be the perfect mother, preparing for every opportunity with my child, made me search out educational toys and the bookcase was piled high with DVDs, toys and books. I was already feeling the pride of the successful woman my baby would, one day, grow into. I knew *she* would make the world a better place – yes, I had discovered on the scans that my baby was a girl. She was so active, constantly kicking, that I often commented what a strong girl our baby would be. I was right; my little Princess has incredible strength, physical and spiritual.

I had been so fascinated by seeing my little girl on a scan that I would have had more and more scans if the hospital had let me, but as there was no problem with my baby, I was only allowed the usual amount! I made many mental plans for my girl. In the culture I was born into, it is not traditional for women to have a strong voice in society, but I knew my daughter would make her mark in the world.

Her daddy was by my side at her birth. I felt drunk on the gas and air, but as soon as my beautiful bouncing baby of seven pounds five ounces arrived, my labour pains quickly disappeared. She stole our hearts instantly with her mop of beautiful curls as her massive brown eyes stared up at her Mummy and Daddy. Her middle name, signifying 'heroine of God,' felt such a blessing as we celebrated our precious and perfect gift from God.

I struggled with breastfeeding, and initially, my baby needed a bottle to supplement my milk supply. Breastfeeding is not automatically easy for all mothers, but I desperately wanted the connection it provides for mother and baby, so I was determined to do the best for my baby, and I persevered, feeding her myself for a couple of years. I experienced the usual baby blues, but we were so happy and thankful that we were now a family of three. I tried to do my best in every situation for my new daughter. My goal has always been to give the best to my children.

Her daddy and I would awaken each morning to Princess's sweet singing as she grew into toddlerhood. *Old Macdonald Had a Farm* was one of her favourite songs, which she sang at the playgroup she loved to attend with her many friends. Of course, she loved all the actions; during the day, when she continually filled our home with her singing, we would join in with her. She was our dancing queen; rhythm and music flowed through her tiny body as she bounced up and down, entertaining us with her lively movements.

I had the pleasure of choosing the preschool, which I thought was the best, and I felt so much joy as her face lit up whenever we entered the classroom each morning. She would skip out to me at the end of each session, clutching one of the many paintings she had enjoyed creating.

Rise and Shine

She would scoot along on her favourite push-along, and when we arrived at the playground, the slides and swings would call her like a duck to water. She would be up and down those slides and then climbing, climbing, climbing! She would scurry down, run over to the playground bicycles and patiently await her turn.

My little girl loved her doll with its masses of hair which she brushed, just as I did hers each day for playgroup. If ever she left her dolly at the nursery, we had to return to collect her; all the staff knew how much she loved that doll. She also had a big cream soft elephant, which she often hugged.

Our three-and-a-half-year-old daughter had never missed a day of preschool through illness because of her exemplary health. She was full of beans and oozed happiness wherever she went. She was popular, and I had made many lovely friends, all mothers of her friends, with whom she communicated well. Her teachers found her one of the brightest children in the creche, always so jolly, beaming away.

I enjoyed every moment of the toddler years of my Princess. My excitement grew as I started to consider a primary school for my daughter. I would discuss the various opportunities with my friends and the mothers of my daughter's playmates.

These formative years remain with me as a firm foundation, which I clung onto even when we walked through the dark valleys when the troubles, which I will share with you, hit us. We managed to climb the mountain back to the summit of happiness, and this book will explain how we found the way. I hope my story will help others encountering their own challenges who might think they cannot face their problems, but my message is that you can.

I shall always recall the moment I first held my precious daughter in my arms as our lives flooded with joy. Equally, I will never forget the days, four years later, when I began to see her tears, the continual floods of tears that let me know something was now terribly wrong. I want to tell my story because it is a story of joy that has survived difficult times.

We were all excited when I discovered that I was pregnant with a baby brother for our Princess, who was overjoyed to be allowed to visit me in the hospital and meet her baby brother. However, on her return home, I noticed she began to cry. Naturally, we thought this was probably the result of being overwhelmed. It can be a big shock for a child to see its mother with a new baby in her arms, although we had prepared her for the new arrival. All sorts of thoughts went through my mind. Had she not realised that, although there was a new baby on its way, a brother, he would share her mummy? Like many parents of a second sibling, we ensured that we made a fuss of our daughter and that any visitors gave her their attention too, but the crying persisted, and the outbursts grew longer and more frequent. We questioned ourselves then – were we pampering her too much, and maybe we should start to reprimand her? Was she attention-seeking? The crying grew worse, to the point that it was intolerable. What were

Florence Yuwimana

we do to? What was happening to our daughter with her sunny disposition? Where had she gone? When would she return to normal? If only we had known then what challenges we were to face.

2

LOVE CAN DRIVE OUT THE FEAR

The tears of our Princess would not stop, day after day. My new beautiful baby boy didn't cry; he was a contented and happy baby, just as our daughter had been. We were so thankful to have been blessed again with the gift of new life, which is always a miracle. Our children were undoubtedly part of a divine purpose, as we believe all children are. New life is more wondrous than we can ever imagine. God had blessed us with our son and daughter, and we felt privileged that our lives had helped to create these wonderful children; we were so happy.

I found it challenging being away from my extended family because I had no local relatives to ask for advice. However, I still appealed to my family and in-laws, though they were abroad, for help and advice when I could not quell our daughter's new crying bouts. My lovely family sent as much advice as they could from across the miles, as did her daddy's family from abroad. They pointed out that in their country, it was the tradition to ask grandparents' or older siblings, aunts or uncles to look after the firstborn for a while as the parents adjust to life with another baby; this reconfirmed my early beliefs that maybe, Princess was crying because she couldn't deal with the attention her new brother was demanding. We gave her all the attention possible, but the crying became aggressive, and her frustration was evident. It was heartbreaking to hear. Any parent who has tried to soothe a crying baby with colic will understand what we were facing; nothing would comfort nor quieten her. She obviously did not have colic,

Rise and Shine

but whatever the problem, it was causing her so much upset.

Princess was no longer the only one constantly in tears as my own soul was upset. I fought to find out where her previous happiness had gone. I had fallen into a nightmare because my daughter was regressing before my eyes. Was I simply imagining it? Was it a temporary illness, an emotional reaction to the new baby? I fired countless questions at myself. During those early months, I could hardly speak through my sobs as I tried to work out why all the changes were happening to my little girl. I had grief in my heart, but at the same time, I wanted to celebrate the joy of my newborn son *and* the presence of our daughter; my despair was overwhelming, and I dared to hope that if things got better, I would one day write a book to guide others unfortunate enough to find themselves on such a horrendous journey.

I could not accept the first signs that something was troubling our beautiful daughter, and I was in complete

Florence Yuwimana

denial. Whenever a thought arose that there was a problem, which didn't seem to go away, I would ignore it. Others were noticing because even if I went to the shops or the park with Princess, the smiley girl everyone had once known was now crying continually. I remember that one day I took her to the park, and she just lay on the path and cried and cried, such a contrast to the girl who had used to ride along to the park as fast as her scoot-along would go. She used to love looking at books with me, but now all she did was destroy them, biting the corners, tearing them up. I used my own pause button frequently, taking a few moments to reflect on what we could be doing wrong. I would take a few deep breaths before engaging with my daughter. I had to remind myself that my goal was to calm my child and not escalate the upset by allowing her to sense my own distress. I was grateful that I did not have to go out to work. I had the opportunity to be there, in the home, for my children and never let go of my desire to build a close, loving and deep relationship with all my children despite

Rise and Shine

what life threw at me. I tried everything I could to connect emotionally with my crying daughter, conscious of the tone of my voice; was it reflecting my warmth to her? I tried to ensure that my message was not just verbal, and also sought ways to display my non-verbal messages – Princess, I will help you; Princess, you are safe. Princess, we can handle this. I thought that the noise of her own tears might upset her, so I tried to use words sparingly – maybe she could not process too many words in her distress. I chose short sentences such as 'I'm right here.' I decided that time must not be an issue; I must show Princess we had all the time in the world to help her.

Eventually, I managed to convince myself. 'Come on, Florence; you can do it!' I commanded myself to rise each morning and shine. I thought -Stand up for your daughter; if you continue to cry and cry, you will solve nothing. I persuaded myself that I must go to the doctor; I must explain all the recent changes in my daughter and face up to the fact that maybe they were not temporary. Like myself, her daddy

Florence Yuwimana

had to work through all this, and he always showed such kind understanding and empathy to our daughter and me. A good father makes all the difference in a child's life – and her daddy is an excellent father. He is a pillar of strength to us all. He goes out to work and supports us all, and we work as a team; we are thankful that our team efforts have now rewarded us with well-adjusted children. He is open-minded, allowing our children to be their own unique individuals. We have both accepted that our children are different but all equally precious. We respect their individuality.

In those early days, it felt like my personal life had frozen, as I only had one focus in mind as I realised that I wanted to do everything in my power to support my little girl, to find answers and hopefully a cure. I knew that everything else, aside my immediate family, would have to go on hold. Before I gave birth to Princess, I had been studying Social Studies, and I rapidly realised that I might not fulfill any ambitions towards a career. The real me had become like a ship lost in a deep fog at sea. I was going round and round in circles inside my head. Not only was I worried about our daughter, but I also became concerned about the effect all this had on me. Where had the social-loving Florence disappeared to? The Florence who loved to go out with her friends and laugh. I did not understand myself anymore. Feeling so down, I did not attract pleasant or happy times anymore. Who wants to spend time with somebody who does nothing but cry; besides, who would I let near me? I was cutting myself off from well-meaning friends. I lost my desire to go out and could see no point in taking care of my appearance. However, my unconditional love for my family sustained me. At this stage, I did not know what to do for my little girl but knew I could continue to say to her, 'I offer you my love freely without any condition.' I held on to the fact that I knew in my heart that this love would see us through these challenging times. I knew I could lean into the tension of all the challenges by continuing to offer connection and love, however down I felt. My love was not depending on any of my children reaching milestones. They

Florence Yuwimana

are all our miracles, unique individuals, and we accept them all as gifts from God.

I found many things difficult; for example, cooking became dangerous as Princess would switch the cooker on and off, and I had to watch her constantly if she followed me into the kitchen. Those words to myself, 'Come on, you can do it,' were my mantra at times like this when I began to realise that our daughter no longer had any safety awareness. We had tried our best to childproof our house for toddlers and babies, so we had a starting point. We had tried to make our home the safest place for our children, allowing them as much freedom as possible. We hoped to guarantee there was no danger of scalding by ensuring Princess would not turn the hot taps on. We tried to identify the top safety risks, and as we became more aware of her predisposition, we could be one step ahead of any hazard she might encounter around our

Rise and Shine

home. Being a parent of a child with no awareness of danger is a challenging and scary job. However, we did our best to make our home safe for all our children, always prepared for the unexpected.

3

FINDING MY INNER STRENGTH

My fear had started. I was in the wilderness. I had to face the truth – I had a baby born normal; at preschool, she had been walking and talking, but unfortunately, once she became four, things had not worked out how I hoped they would. My fear developed then because I was still learning to be a mother, but now, I faced a challenge to turn my fear around. I was scared to face this fear and didn't want to accept it. It was an internal battle for me. I feared how I would explain this change to everyone who knew Princess. How could I now describe that she has turned into someone else? I started

Florence Yuwimana

trying to explain to people, one at a time. I feared they judged me as they thought, 'What have you done to this child?'

As each challenge reared its head, I felt myself becoming weaker and weaker. The first challenge was the constant aggressive crying, followed by the challenge of the pure frustration which my previously smiling girl was facing.

The next challenge is what I shall call 'the events,' when Princess seemed to nod off to sleep suddenly in the middle of the day. Her head would suddenly drop forward as if she was dozing. The crying persisted but appeared terror-struck as if having a nightmare in the middle of the day. I wondered if she was having nightmares in the evening and then reliving them during the day, so I started to sleep beside her to see if I could sense this was the case.

The next challenge was that she became an insomniac and was not sleeping through the night. Some days I could not believe I was still alive due to my exhaustion because, don't forget, I also had a newborn baby. I was confused as to which

Rise and Shine

child to attend to and when. Of course, her daddy helped, but he had a job to go to each day, and he needed his sleep to function adequately and continue to support us all.

Attending my little boy needed to be a soothing experience for him, so I tried not to be tense and anxious over what Princess was up to. She would not lie in her bed if she was not asleep and would wander around; this created further huge safety issues as she sometimes turned the taps on, so we designed ways to prevent this from happening. Princess began to choose seclusion, sitting in a corner, not wishing to be close to us. She began to reject me carrying or hugging her. Something within me made me realise it was my job to get up each morning, seeing each day as a fresh start, and to do something for my daughter, to never give up on hope.

Princess began to pick at her food, her large and healthy appetite replaced by a desire for chips. Meal times became difficult because she no longer interacted with us. It was as if she needed her own space.

Florence Yuwimana

Our daughter's speech was disappearing; I no longer heard the precious call of 'Mummy'. She had lost interest in all her toys apart from those which lit up and played music.

It took my mother's initiative to work out if my girl felt physically unwell. With each passing month and then years, new challenges popped up; for example, in later years, I decided to take her to the dentist – I had prepared by brushing her teeth twice daily and then allowing her to hold her own toothbrush. Our trip to the dentist was a comical disaster. The dentist and dental nurses were very kind but had not experienced assisting a child with special needs. Princess did not understand all their requests to sit in the chair and was wandering around, touching all the dials and fiddling with all the equipment. I tried to get her to open her mouth by saying, 'Aah,' and hoping she would copy, but the dentist never really got to inspect her teeth despite his best efforts. It was not the fault of him or his staff, but it just highlighted the continued problems we were facing. When the time came for Princess to lose her baby teeth, I was petrified that she would swallow them. I was so thankful when I found them on her pillow each morning.

I saw it as my job to rise each day and show her the love I felt, but I also had to keep searching for my inner strength. I had good grounding because I can honestly say that my childhood had been happy, happy, happy – not due to the possessions we had but due to the family we were. My family always met my social, emotional and educational needs. We were always playing, singing, reading and talking, and I was determined, as was her daddy, to create such an uplifting atmosphere in our home. Children need happy parents, and we ensured that we found ways to let go of our concerns for Princess, but, of course, as you are reading, this did not happen overnight. We learnt to bounce back from setbacks and to make plans to create a path to move forward positively, never forgetting that we had to allow her to be as independent as possible, despite the strict limitations. These were all the thoughts and realisations I had when I came to a point I

Florence Yuwimana

could work them out, but before that time, I faced my inner darkness of mind and spirit.

I had to recognise the spirit within me by constantly telling myself I was strong and I could do this. I had to find a suitable place to weep but then wipe my tears and tell myself I was better than this weak, crying woman. I knew I was trying to erect a barrier to protect myself from the pity I imagined I saw in the faces of the other parents. I now realise that they just wanted to help and support me, they are lovely, considerate people, but I became too blinded by my stress to see things clearly. In a way, I had become my own enemy.

No one can steal our emotions, spirituality or happiness unless we allow it to happen. Nobody could hurt my personality but me. I had always been very sociable with many friends, a person full of excitement, and always ready to party, but I came to lose that. I could not smile anymore; it felt like a needle protruded in my chest. My own approach and mindset to everything had created sickness in me, not through food, but through feeding myself with negativity. I had to sort myself out before I could truly reach out and help others. I did not want to go out; I didn't want to meet people. I was trapping myself in a downward spiral. I thought people were peculiarly looking at me, although I now know it was all in my mind, caused by stress. I was not smiling at anyone, and understandably, people were not smiling back, or at least, I could not see their smiles because of my negativity. I had always been joyful, but now I felt nobody wanted to spend time with me. Looking back, it was my depression because I now understand that all my lovely friends and the other parents were trying their best to help me, but I was blind to them because of the downward spiral I had fallen into. I can now say, from experience, that nobody can support you if you can't help yourself. I could go to the great psychologist but couldn't hear what they were saying to me, not due to any hearing problem but the upset in my heart. I had put myself in a cage in which I wanted to stay. I wanted people to leave me alone. I had to battle the voices of negative thoughts and order them to vacate.

Florence Yuwimana

Princess helped me to find my inner strength because I looked at her and saw her beauty, my beautiful daughter who just needed me to find a way to help her. Everyone had become a problem to me because I was rejecting everybody who was trying to help. I could not accept their love and care because of the mental distress I was drowning in.

I needed to practice self-awareness to build my inner strength. I needed to give myself time to develop my patience. Looking at my beautiful daughter, I found the mindset to pursue growth. I was starting on a journey of rediscovering myself inspired by the needs of my lovely Princess. If I could rediscover myself, I would be able to help her. I needed to find a positive mood, inner peace, and determination and to let my love flow through to my perfect daughter.

4

Happiness is not Based on What we Have

I believe that, in contrast to my childhood, people now have too many possessions that blind them to what is significant in life – family, friends, love, and spending quality time together, and that is why we always eat together as a family. We need to listen to each other and speak over mealtimes with no television distracting us. My advice to families is to make time for each other. Today's world is full of too many busy, busy people.

I realised this world is not entirely friendly, and anything can happen. This world presents many surprises to us, some good, some awful! I also learnt that everybody messes up, but

Florence Yuwimana

we must move forward. I really did have to see life as a glass half full, not half empty.

I realised that I needed to look at the positives in my life and note things I could be thankful for. I was grateful that Princess had no physical disabilities. I was grateful she could see and walk, that she was strong.

I had to use my mother's initiative to discover what my daughter might require. My efforts, patience, love, and time have enabled me to be in tune with her, and I can now read her needs. We communicate by our hearts, and nowadays, I can even tell if she has had a bad day at school. If she has a cold threatening, she will come and lie on my knee. She has good immunity, so she is not often ill. We never hide things from our children, so they must be brave and accept medicine time which we always make as pleasurable as possible, and if Princess needs any medication, she will take it.

I had to develop my own philosophy for moving forward, so I could help Princess more and more. I continually reminded myself, 'Rise and Shine,' each morning when all I wanted to do was stay in bed so I would fight to get up. Her daddy and I treat our children equally; we have no difference in our approach, whether they are a boy or a girl. Sometimes it has been felt that women have had a lesser voice in some societies than men, but I knew that I must rise and become the voice for Princess. Yet again, I said to myself, 'Come on, Florence, you can do this.' You can stand for your daughter because nobody else but her father and I can. I found my motivation as her mother and as one woman fighting to give another female a stronger voice in the world. Her daddy has always supported the children and me and understood my desire to make the path smoother for Princess and her difficulties. He has always ensured that he spends quality time with each of the children. He is excellent at getting them involved in sports and will find ways to help our daughter participate. He leads us all by a good example.

Overcoming my depression did not happen overnight. As I am sharing, overcoming the negative behaviours surrounding

Florence Yuwimana

my depression did not happen instantly. So, I developed my philosophies to help keep me on track as I rose to climb my mountain. I imagined two choices I had; negative or positive. All the negative behaviours would wake me each morning, but I rose daily and told myself to avoid anger and depression. I tried to reject all the times I felt anger against the situation and the people surrounding me. Then, I got tempted to seek trouble from those I loved and respected. I'd feel disappointed in my closest family and friends, wrongly believing they did not understand my upset. I would complain. By keeping away from these negative thoughts, my poorer behaviours would diminish. I knew I was hurting others and myself if I wandered into the path of negativism.

I needed to find all the positive aspects of my personality that I previously had before I had fallen into depression. I needed to reassess my aims and knew that if I could achieve them, I would best be able to help and support Princess on her journey in life. My objectives contained agreeableness – being kind, sympathetic and helpful to others. I aimed for better emotional intelligence – empathy, self-awareness and inclusivity; I knew I had to be conscientious to ensure I tried every door to get correct medical and educational help for our daughter. At first, I denied our daughter's condition and would not go to the doctor because I could not accept what was happening to her. I decided to keep to the positive and my objective of honesty – never denying to myself or others the truth about Princess's challenges. I wanted confidence to enable me to speak up for her. I needed the optimism of positivity to maintain hope even in the darkest hours. Compassion would be necessary for Princess, and towards the effect all the stress had on the rest of the family and the need to recognise how much others were trying their best to help me. I aimed for friendliness to regain my former jolly, open, warm smile when I was a friend to all. I needed the ambition to see all my goals to completion – not mine, but the ones I hoped to score for my daughter. I needed to be humble and not fall into self-praise when I saw progress, and I needed to be flexible, to adapt, to be able and willing to see the points and suggestions of others, and not to think that my way was the only way. All these positive tributes, and more, lay in my decision to persevere. Of course, it was not easy – some days, I would run back into negativity, and it could take a couple of days of determination to get back to a positive outlook, to rise and shine once more. Self-love is the foundation of mental health, and I knew that reaching for the right mindset would enable me to like and love myself again, which was necessary for helping our daughter. This positive approach lifted me from the low place where I could not see the wood for the trees. I knew I had to reconnect with the people I had kept my distance from. I needed to stay in touch with people and become more active again. I needed to face my fears and find a routine.

I learnt that appearances were not as important as what was inside my mind, heart and body. The positive approach would set me free from the tendency to dwell on my problems and to look and search for good things each day. A smile from our daughter was the reward for keeping to that determination.

I needed to watch my diet and eat good foods as I knew diet could hugely impact psychological and mental states.

I kept a diary in which I wrote a few lines each night, 'Florence, you are not going into the negative path tomorrow, and it will be a good day. You will smile.' Each night I would set myself that goal no matter what!

I had counselling, and I know many people find it beneficial, but I did not find the questions were the ones that led me to open up. I needed the time to get to the stage where I could recognise that I had to overcome things myself, but most importantly, I had to want to my anger, and my refusal to cooperate made me drop out of the sessions. I need to stress that it was not the fault of the counsellors, but it just did not work for me with the mindset I had developed. I believe counselling can be beneficial and life-saving, but I was not ready to engage.

5

FACING A MOUNTAIN

.

O nce I began to climb the mountain, I had to be wary of the pitfalls. Inferiority and negative thoughts could create fear to rob my confidence. By not facing the reality of my daughter's illness, decision-making would be challenging for me. It was a battle I had to confront all the time – that I could do better than this. I must accept the situation and do something positive about it. I told myself those circumstances must not determine my future. I had to become the changer of my own life. I could not let suffering be the end of my life. I told myself I must develop an invigorated heart and mind to water my hope and

Florence Yuwimana

to mix with people who would help my hope to grow. Yes, I would finally admit that things have not worked out how I had hoped, but I'm not giving up – I'm going forward. I'm not allowing what is inside me to die. I am sharing my story because I want others to follow these discoveries. A challenge accelerates us to a different level of life. It's impossible to go through such a situation as I did and to remain the same person. Moments of shame might have filled our hearts with pain and bitterness, but we do not have to stay in that place forever; we can do better than that.

Social media was helpful in many ways and obviously essential, at times, as I began to search for medical and educational help for Princess. However, I believe social media can take humanity away from us; it can become a source of judgement and prejudice through stereotyping. It can become like gossip or instigate trouble and falsehoods. Social media can take the warmth of friendship away from us, and I found it much more helpful to sit with someone face-to-face than to communicate over social media.

Rise and Shine

From the experiences I have been through, my advice now would be to provide a listening ear if you see someone struggling as I was. I would say to give the person time, sit with them, and if they are not yet at a point where they can share their troubles, then sit in silence, letting them know you are there. Send a gentle message, and don't always expect an answer. I lost many friends because I did not accept their outstretched hands. It could have been pride, I am unsure, but I made no effort to return their kind calls.

I knew I had to fight to get an assessment for my daughter. At first, when I approached the doctor and then the hospital, I felt invisible, anonymous, and just a statistic to deal with. I wanted to pour my heart out to them, to explain exactly how my daughter had changed, but I was at a point where I did not think that their pre-set questions prevented them from listening to the real me. Sometimes, the accents were difficult to understand, and I didn't feel they saw me as a person in my own right. I had to gain my confidence and voice as I wondered if they would have listened more if I had

Florence Yuwimana

been a man or more sure of myself. I had to stand up and speak to my spirit, 'I am a human, facing a mountain, but I will climb it. It was a very steep mountain with many false peaks because I would think I was getting somewhere when I realised there were even more professionals to face – there were nurses, doctors, psychologists, counsellors, therapists and the Department of Education. They were all lovely people, but I was not in the right state of mind to truly comprehend and appreciate their medical methodology or understand the medical terms and jargon. I was shaking with fear, my eyes full of tears. I had to change my mindset – I am not just a typical woman; I must face professional people. I felt small and low, so I had to control my mind. I had to raise my hope higher again and remember, yet again, not to give hope to the negative side of life.

I was unhappy, at first, with the general practitioner because I wondered if he was acknowledging that there was a problem. I did not seem able to get him to understand my concerns. I started to keep a journal about everything that concerned

Rise and Shine

me, but he did not appear as interested as I expected. Again, I wish to say that the doctor was professional; however, I did not see things as intended in my turmoil.

Bewildered, I sought help at the health clinic, where they made an appointment for our daughter to see a children's doctor. I was so happy when one eventually came through, and I met the lady doctor. It was a great relief when she recognised all I was talking about and agreed to refer us to the hospital, although the waiting list was a year. I had been living with the hope that the doctor would solve the problem, but I felt that, yet again, I was having questions fired at me about my pregnancy with my daughter. Maybe I was too impatient, I wanted all the answers, but the doctors obviously were the professionals, but I could not always see that due to my stress. I cried as I gave each answer, trying to convince the doctor that previously, she had been a perfectly normal child. The doctor didn't examine her, which is what I had been expecting. Maybe my expectations were wrong, but I became blinded by my desire to get more immediate

Florence Yuwimana

answers. I was frustrated that I just seemed to be asked more questions. When did she first talk? When did she start to walk? This was not what I wanted. I wanted to be the one to ask the questions and for them to give me the answers. The doctors were doing what was needed, but I was not in the mental space to cooperate professionally.

One of the problems, at first, was that I was still articulating with a broken heart. I was not getting my message across accurately through all my tears; I had to realise that speaking to a psychologist concerning my daughter's welfare was not helpful if I saw it as a place to cry and share my sorrows. I had to continually remind myself to find the mindset to go in and demand the correct help I thought my daughter needed. The doctors decided they would perform hearing tests and declared that she was deaf in one ear. I felt frustrated as I thought they ignored my observational knowledge that she could definitely hear. For example, if I put her favourite music on at home, the theme tune from *Peppa Pig*, she would run

Rise and Shine

downstairs as fast as her legs would carry her. However, if I sat close to her and said her name, I would not get a response.

At each appointment, I became convinced that I faced useless questions. I must have appeared ignorant, but I did not want all those senseless questions which were irrelevant as far as I was concerned. I wanted somebody to check out my little girl physically to examine her brain, her mind. I wanted them to scan her head or something, offer a remedy. I didn't know what I wanted, apart from a cure for whatever was wrong. I needed them to do something to get her back to peak health and happiness, but that was not the case. After the third trip to the hospital, I thought, 'I'm not bringing her here again.' Looking back now, from my good mental state, I appreciate that the medical professionals were doing a good job and they were not at fault.

However, when the doctor heard my complaints, she suggested a referral to another doctor, which showed they were listening to me. I pondered over the offer, wondering

Florence Yuwimana

if I should take the gamble because the next doctor could still not deal with things how I wanted them to. I felt like I was banging my head against a brick wall as I was getting nowhere. After discussions with her daddy, we decided to try the new doctor.

6

ACCEPTING THE LOVE

I thought it might help readers if I shared the therapies I created to help my daughter. So many people, seeing the progress in Princess, have asked me what treatments we received. The answer is clear – we had none – we created our own. Our daughter would be in a different place today if I did not focus on trying to listen or work out what her actions were telling me. I concentrated on finding ways to ensure she understood that we all cherished her as such an integral member of our family. Her daddy was supportive and loyal throughout, accepting my suggestions on what we should do for her. The good father he is, her daddy has always been a

Florence Yuwimana

public defender of his daughter. He protects her and the rest of our family, doing whatever he can to keep us out of harm's way. His unconditional love shines through to us all.

My first step was to get myself better so that I could help Princess. When the crying persisted, I carried her on my back in a sling made from towels. I wanted her to feel my continual physical presence to accentuate that I was there for her. My children are all tall for their age, so it was not easy having a nearly four-year-old on my back. I thought she might see through this action that she was still my baby, even though I now had her brother. I would perform my household tasks and clean with her on my back. Miraculously, the crying subsided and eventually stopped when I carried her everywhere on my back, despite it being physically draining.

I discovered that she loved bubbles, which helped her focus as her eyes followed them; she had lost the ability to make eye contact, so this was one way to try to reverse this. The bubbles engaged her, and later I discovered how they were helping her to communicate with me because she would find a way of letting me know that she wanted extra bubbles. She became fascinated as we blew them and popped them. I could engage her by naming the objects the bubbles were landing on. I could help her understand sharing and taking turns when I let my toddler son have a go instead of me. Bubbles are mesmerising for all, and the different colours would sparkle and attract her attention; I loved seeing her eyes follow the bubbles across the room. I could hide the wand and see if she would make eye contact and turn to look for it, or I could replace the cap and wait to see her reaction – if she wanted the activity to continue. We could have giggles if I purposefully made a mistake and tried to blow bubbles with the cap still on. The bubbles encouraged social interaction with her brothers.

I always believed the answer was to show my daughter more love, to demonstrate my parenting to her, ensuring that she had my attention just as much as my newborn son. I knew millions of pounds of money would not have helped her, but

Florence Yuwimana

being there for her would. My love brought her back from the corners where she sat, absolutely terrified. My constant love retrieved her from that corner; it had needed me to sit beside her every time she cried, comforting her,

Yet again, the words, 'Princess, it is OK, Mummy is here for you,' were uttered by me time and time again. At first, she would not welcome me, but I just gave her the space she needed, and I would sit at a comfortable distance away from her. Eventually, I got her to accept me. During the first few weeks, I considered approaching the tears with, 'Stop this; this is too much.' However, when I understood she had problems, I knew I had to be there with her, give her all my heart, and surround her every moment with love. Discipline was not the answer then, although her daddy and I ensure all our children know the boundaries and family rules; we explain things to our children and chat reasons through, guiding them clearly as to what is a kind action and what is not. We have healthy discipline strategies which work for our family. We always use calm words to tell them what is

Rise and Shine

right and wrong. We set limits with clear and consistent rules that we know the children can follow. We tailor these to the needs of each child. We give consequences, and they understand that with Princess, these might vary. We always let our children know we hear them; listening to them is crucial. We watch for patterns of misbehaviour; for example, could jealousy be causing an issue? We would talk about this rather than give the consequences. We check that our children understand what we are saying. We reinforce and notice good behaviours. We catch them doing good things, and then we can give them genuine and sincere praise. If they are doing something which isn't dangerous, we might choose to ignore it. We redirect poor behaviour if we sense it is from frustration. I recall much from my upbringing, and our extended family and friends share what has worked for them, and we share with them what has worked for us. Our children are well-behaved, happy, loving and kind, so we do not need much discipline.

Florence Yuwimana

I needed to retrain Princess to walk, so I would hold her hand and encourage her. I would make her rise out of the pushchair and walk. Her mind does not coordinate with her body since 'the change,' so I had to guide her on how to eat again and put food in her mouth; there are so many skills that she has lost, and I have had to help her relearn them. It was hard to acknowledge that this would not happen overnight, and I had to work hard on developing patience and aiming for small steps. It was a moment of joy when she learnt to hold a spoon again, although she prefers finger foods!

I spent many hours trying to think of things which might spark interest in her; I noticed that playing in the bath seemed to calm her, so I took her to the swimming baths. She loved the pool. I have to take support with me, a specialised teacher, and we go during non-public sessions. She has not learnt to swim, but she adores splashing away. We attend weekly, and she always sleeps much better since starting these sessions. When she had stopped sleeping, the doctors prescribed some medication, but I did not want my little girl drugged up, so I tried to think of alternatives, and swimming did the trick.

She loves trampolines, but if we were ever to get one, we all know that she would not wish to get off it! She would want to sleep on it! Besides, the doctor told us it would have the opposite effect of calming her down, and we do not want that! She loves the fairy lights which decorate her bedroom and all the sparkly things, so Christmas is a great time of happiness for Princess with all the glittery ornaments and the mass of lights everywhere!

She loves the shakers I make, loaded with rice, and the tubs I fill with different products for her to feel the variety, for example, a bucket of beads or sand. She enjoys it when I fill vessels with coloured water for her to play with.

Once, we had home teachers for her, but finding the right teacher and expenses caused some problems. Sometimes they would attend for ten hours per week, but the teacher's personality needed to suit her; otherwise, we would see her

Florence Yuwimana

regress. I would buy jigsaws with the alphabet on them and educational toys. I discovered that if her brother sat and played, we would catch her paying the odd moment of attention to what we were doing. I tried to sing songs that might have some educational influence, but teaching traditional subjects like English and maths seemed out of the question at first.

I attended a speech and language course, learning sign language and how to use the pictures, but Princess would turn away when I tried to use these, so I adapted all I learnt to the methods I found she would respond to. I discovered how we could communicate, and I would let her stand by me as I prepared her a drink. Eventually, she found her unique way of letting me know what she wanted and when; it was just a matter of tuning in to how she wished to communicate with me. For example, if I change her bedtime routine, she will let me know, in her own way, that I have done things in an incorrect order; if I put her shoes on the wrong feet, she will let me know. She will let me know she wants more of her favourite fruit – grapes. She likes chocolate but not as much as her grapes!

7

REACHING OUT

I was blessed to have a strong upbringing which had prepared the foundations for me to cope with the battles life has thrown at me during the last six years. I look back at my childhood Christmas celebrations, and I do not see a mountain of gifts but an abundance of love as the extended family visited us, and I see the genuine joy of the Christian message. I have tried to recapture this approach to life in my own family.

In the early days, some of the mothers of my daughter's friends came around to offer help; they could see that I was out of my mind, just crying all the time. All I had wanted to

Florence Yuwimana

do was look at photos of when Princess was healthy, just a few months before. Seeing the other mothers reminded me of the happy playdates we enjoyed together. I found it challenging to explain to these parents that my daughter was now a different child when I did not know why. She had been playing in the park with her friends, going to their homes, but suddenly she wanted nothing to do with them; equally, I wanted nothing to do with the parents because I was hurting inside my heart so badly. The anguish was unbearable, and it was tough to see the other small children still living life to the full as my girl had done until very recently. I couldn't bear to be around the children or their parents, so naturally, I lost many friends. I now know they understood and tried their best, but to be fair, nothing they could do would help relieve my huge burden of sorrow and grief. I also wondered what on earth they might be saying behind my back. I also had some pride and did not want to cry in front of them. I was not ready or able to share with them the experience I was going through.

Her daddy is sporty and would take Princess to the park with a ball. He would tell her constantly that she was a big girl, and he would persevere even when she showed no interest. He was so kind to her, setting no time limits, his patience never-ending, and it paid off as she now has some hand-eye coordination. He taught her to use her scooter and helped to rekindle her passion for energetic activities in the park. She always loves her sport time with her daddy.

I decided to take Princess to spend time with my extended family, and all my worries about how she would cope on the plane subsided when she settled by the window, enthralled by the clouds. My family spoilt her rotten, and she blossomed in the love and care of her aunts, uncles and grandparents; I know that if we ever moved there, I could return to work because my marvellous family would sort the childminding between them. However, we are settled here, where all the children have friends, as do we. Her daddy has steady employment, and we value the support of our church and the children's schools.

Florence Yuwimana

When my daughter was eight, I gave birth to my second son. Our family is happy, and all the children are protective of each other. Our eldest son tries to teach his sister but can get frustrated, but she responds more to his teaching than she does mine! She is protective of her brothers, and if ever I have to reprimand them, she will stand before me and try to stop me from speaking firmly to them!

I always encourage my sons to have their own life and time with their friends; there was a stage when my eldest son began copying his sister's mannerisms and behaving like her, so we facilitated his social life. I deliberately sent him to a different preschool than the one that Princess had attended; it would have been too painful for me, but more importantly, I did not know how it would affect her when we dropped her brother off if he had gone to the one, she had attended, and I did not want my son starting school under the shadow of all the troubles we had encountered. We all deserved a fresh start.

Rise and Shine

We threw a party for our eldest son at the local cinema, hiring it with others for about 50 friends. That was Princess's first trip to the cinema, which she enjoyed, and it worked well as we let all the children wander around if they wanted.

Our eldest boy went through a stage where he had many questions to ask concerning his sister's learning difficulties. He wanted to know why she didn't have to follow all the rules as he did, why she didn't have to say thank you! He understood that we must be patient and help her comprehend as she cannot communicate. We always try to be honest. We hide nothing from our children. When he was about three, our eldest son had a few months when he tried to be in charge of his sister, and I had to hold her hand and help her to force him back if he tried pushing her around. Explaining to him what a kind girl she was, seemed to do the trick, and now it is lovely to see the loving relationship that all my children have. 'Be kind to one another and share' has been my message to them, which all three now put into practice.

8

LEARNING TO SMILE AGAIN

Thank God, the new doctor was brilliant; she listened to me, and I could see she genuinely wanted to discover the cause of our daughter's problems. At last, I heard the words I wanted to hear-she would perform all the tests necessary to try to make a diagnosis. She was intrigued when I told her our daughter was born a perfectly healthy child. She asked me to keep a record of each time that she fell. She suspected seizures, but the resulting tests did not support this theory. The new doctor understood and appreciated how I worked. She showed great compassion, and I discovered I could explain myself fully to her. She was

Florence Yuwimana

full of praise and empathy, acknowledging that she did not know how I had managed to cope and get to this point. My heaviness of heart began to lift when she spoke with me. I felt I could breathe once more.

Then, even though the new doctor was helpful and understanding, I was still not entirely healthy. My depression meant I was not cooperating, but the brilliant doctor understood this, accepting that I was going through a tough time. She allowed me to behave as I was. She provided me with a social worker at the hospital who took on some of the tasks I had been wading through, contacting some of the other professionals for me.

The doctor looked abroad for advice. All the tests returned, marked normal. It was incredibly challenging for me to accept the doctor's decision- that there is no known name for our daughter's condition – and therefore, she was diagnosed as normal when clearly, she now has disabilities. I got to the stage where I did not want a label for my daughter's illness.

Rise and Shine

The report was full of things she could not do that a child her age should be able, but she still got marked as normal. I eventually came to terms with the fact that I would need to stop looking for a diagnosis; it was taking too much out of me, constantly searching for a name for this terrible illness that had struck our lives.

It has been like a full-time job, constantly fighting for a suitable school for Princess. I could not begin to estimate the number of letters I had written to various officials and the number of forms I had struggled to complete; always, at least one required a piece of information I needed to research. I looked for national sources of advice because it was a battle to get a statement, an acknowledgement of her need for special education. To get a statement, we needed a Statutory Assessment; this involved many professionals looking at her special educational needs, and they needed to decide what aid she required for those needs. Because I had withdrawn her from her school, I did not have the support of an educational establishment to offer supporting

Florence Yuwimana

evidence, such as endorsements and lists of incidents which made typical school education impossible for Princess. I needed teachers to guide me as to the educational goals she would require. I needed evidence of her behaviours and needs, but as she spent most of her time with me, there were no others to report on the challenges she presented and the reasons why she could not attend a typical school. I needed to make informed decisions because there were many crucial deadlines to be aware of and the request for many professional reports. I needed guidance to help me state her educational needs clearly and precisely so there would be no confusion or difference in interpretation. Not having a medical diagnosis of her condition was a massive hurdle. I needed to convince the education board that she needed an assessment. The whole process demanded extensive research and an organised approach. It needed a clear mind, and as you will have realised, this was an impossibility in the first few months of the trauma, as much evidence was required to support my request. The objectives of the special educational

Rise and Shine

provision had to be set out clearly and specifically for every type of challenging behaviour displayed. There were appeals to organise as I fought my way through the process. The timelines were often subject to change, and each part of the process took many months. We knew that we did not want residential care for our daughter.

When I finally received a list of schools, there were still hours of research as I waded through each. I needed a school name for the statement to show where our daughter's needs would be best met. I always felt that the professionals were all running away from the situation because I felt alone without the support of a teacher's report.

9

RISING FROM THE VALLEY

If you see Princess today, you would not believe she has problems because she has no physical disabilities. All you will see is a pretty girl with the loveliest eyes. I cut her beautiful hair myself when necessary, but she likes to wear it long now and will happily sit while I style her hair, although, for some unknown reason, she does not like having her nails cut. She will hide the nail clippers! I have to check her shoes regularly, checking their fit to avoid sore toes as she is going through a growth spurt.

We seemed to be getting nowhere with our applications for a school for Princess. I had to acquire the virtue of patience,

Florence Yuwimana

not a natural attribute of mine! A friend recommended that I look for a solicitor. We searched for the best solicitor with relevant experience and expertise in educational needs. I showed him all the files of documentation I had kept from my efforts to attain a place in a specialised school. I poured my heart out to him, and he agreed to take the case; we paid the money, and I kept thinking, 'I am crazy,' when the solicitor suggested we take this to court. I felt out of depth because I'd never had anything to do with a court. It felt like a mad situation to be going to the high court. I was just an innocent mother speaking up for her child, so I wondered how I had gotten into this situation. I felt that I had fallen into boiling water as now I sensed negativity in some words. I thought I had provided all the correct information, but the legal terms could be confusing. I had been so hopeful that, at last, somebody else would fight for me. I had thought, 'Hallelujah,' so it was a massive shock in the February of 2021 when a letter fell through my letterbox informing me that the case had been dropped from the court.

However, I did obtain a list of the available schools, and the solicitor advised me to contact some. However, some were not open. A helpful lady came to my rescue; she emailed the solicitor for me and took over. I felt that I had come to the end of the road, having sent letters to anybody I could, pleading for a place for my child. I had tried everything, so I was thankful to the three ladies who helped me. I was at a point of exhaustion. I could not understand how a judge and solicitor failed to see the situation as I really was. Why could they not do what was so obviously best for our child? Where they failed, the power of these three women who came into my life at the right moment to help succeeded. The passion of these women was brilliant. It was their determination which won a place at school for our daughter.

When I finally received the letter telling me our daughter had a place at school, I cried with delight. I was ecstatic and rang the three ladies, screaming, 'You have changed our daughter's life!' Her daddy and I were very grateful.

Florence Yuwimana

There was a bit of a blip in the May when I received another letter retracting the offer of a place! You can imagine my tears and howls. The school said the problem was that there were insufficient teachers. A night did not pass where I did not email the school, reminding them of the need to find a place for Princess. I was the strong voice for my girl. Therefore, we had to wait for the following September. I told you I have had to learn patience!

The School and I now have a great relationship, and we are more than happy with the school, but most importantly, our daughter is happy, happy, happy.

Gone are the days when I don't like people to ask me about our daughter's condition. She adores music and particularly enjoys the piano and drums. We love listening to her banging on our piano; it is a brilliant exercise for her hands. We are searching for the right piano teacher for her. Our daughter will make it clear if she feels comfortable with someone. She is always calmer after her music sessions. The new etch-a-sketch

Rise and Shine

is another favourite item with her, although all the children love to take turns on it too; my children share well.

Her daddy is a fabulous father and will happily look after the children now that I have regained a social life. I might go for a swim or coffee with friends, and I would like to take this opportunity to thank all my friends for their love and support throughout the difficult years and for waiting patiently for me until I was ready to embrace life again. They know I have found positivity out of the traumas and will not let negativity rule me any more.

10

HOPE, THE MOTHER OF SUCCESS

We will probably celebrate with a Princess-styled cake from our favourite bakery when our daughter celebrates her birthday. I can confirm now that happiness does not derive from what we have; if it did, I would not have the smile on my face that I now constantly wear. Our situation has not changed, but we have. My children exhale happiness, and I feel that I have imparted the glories of my delightful childhood to them. They are happy because of who they are. Her daddy has been my rock, and all the success I now describe is due to his efforts as much as my own.

Florence Yuwimana

Princess is calm nowadays and will enjoy flicking through the pages of a book, particularly if it contains pictures of nature or people. Colourful images attract her. She loves to sit in front of the television and sing along to any musical programmes – she does not have a vocabulary, but in her own way, she will participate with the songs; her all-time favourite is *Twinkle Twinkle Little Star*. Occasionally, we imagine we hear the odd word when she might repeat something that has just been said, for example, 'Merry Christmas'. My heart bursts with joy, hoping she might, one day, say, 'Mama'. However, our daughter can never disappoint us; she truly is our miracle child who has bonded us all into the loving family unit we are. We would have her no other way. Life is good to us as we celebrate all the achievements of our daughter, and she has shown us the meaning of the phrase, 'Things come in cans, not in can'ts' We have celebrated many steps of progress, but our primary contentment is that Princess is happy and knows we love her and we know she loves us. She learnt to hug back and enjoy our hugs and kisses, which is a massive achievement when we recall how she wanted nothing to do with us and no physical contact.

Princess has been at her new school since September, and we often walk there. Having dropped her brother off at his school many times, she took well to being left with her six new classmates. But she is happy with her new friends. It is incredible to see that our little girl is sociable again. Her teachers constantly remark on what a kind girl she is. Just the other day, a fellow boy classmate ran out without his coat, so she took it out for him. We sometimes fear that due to her vulnerability, she might get bullied, but the teachers look out for her, and her brothers are very protective, although they will always be at different schools from her.

It is a dream come true as we are delighted with the specialised school, which teaches her independence. It is hard to acknowledge that, before she was ill, she was capable of more than she is now. She knew her alphabet and could count to ten. She was so advanced for her age as I prepared lessons

Florence Yuwimana

with her every morning. However, we have no regrets. We see the unique individual she is, and the hope I once had when I was pregnant with my daughter – that she would make her mark on the world – is coming true. She is loved by all who come into contact with her and an inspiration to all with her contentment and joy of spirit.

She can show excitement, and everybody notices when her Daddy picks her up from school as a special treat because her reaction is so happy. Princess now only cries if she feels pain which is a big sign of progress. Those frustrated tears of long ago are in the distant past, and it is tears of joy we now sometimes shed when we see yet another step of progress in the life of our beautiful daughter. I count my blessings daily, and I am thankful that our daughter can walk; I am grateful that she can see. I am appreciative that she is physically strong. I am thankful that she is as she is. When I took her to visit, my family were overjoyed to see and hear that all is going well in our daughter's life – such a contrast to the times I had asked them for help in those early days.

Rise and Shine

I have a strong Christian belief and have felt supported throughout by my church, but I would say to my readers that the thing that has helped me the most is having faith in and believing in myself. I am not some superwoman, and anybody reading this book, whatever age, can rise up if they believe in themselves. That is one of my messages to you all.

I love to go to church. I used to take Princess, and she was always greatly welcomed into the community and showed great love. The church was very supportive, but I found it difficult because she preferred to walk around rather than sit in the congregation. I now see people from the church once a week for fellowship, a social get-together and bible study. We might discuss the message from the previous Sunday's fellowship. I feel that much of our daughter's progress is due to the prayers from the faithful members of our church.

Nowadays, I feel like shouting for joy as I look at my miracle child. My upbringing, my determination, her daddy, my doctors, her teachers, and my Christian faith have all

Florence Yuwimana

combined to bring us to this point where I can write this book to share the message of 'Rise and Shine' each day with the joy of knowing you can find happiness if you search it out.

My joy of spirit as I celebrate the first decade of life with my miracle child is abundant. As I close my book, I hope you can join in with my praise and thanks that our precious daughter is in our lives.

Our family life is good, and our love for each other will endure forever. Princess is our miracle child, as are her two brothers. We have all learnt to rise and shine, facing whatever the day throws at us. I hope my book will encourage you to find your own way to happiness. Hold on in there and believe in yourself. One day you will get up and rise and shine again.